Hank Aaron

Hank Aaron
by Bill Gutman

A THISTLE BOOK

Published by
GROSSET & DUNLAP, INC.
New York

For Beth, with thanks

The author would like to thank Bob Hope of the Atlanta Braves Publicity Department and Mrs. Estella Aaron for their help in providing material for this book.

PICTURE CREDITS: Wide World, pages 68–9, 84; Atlanta Braves, pages ii, viii, 2, 3, 40, 72–3; United Press International, pages 23, 34, 49, 60, 62–3, 66–7, 75, 76–7, 82–3.

Copyright © 1973 by Bill Gutman
All Rights Reserved
Published Simultaneously in Canada
Library of Congress Catalog Card No. 72-92927
ISBN: 0-448-21471-7 (trade edition)
ISBN: 0-448-26234-7 (library edition)
Printed in the United States of America

CONTENTS

Chapter 1   1
Chapter 2   14
Chapter 3   31
Chapter 4   44
Chapter 5   59
Statistics   86

Hank Aaron

CHAPTER 1

Hank Aaron wanted to be a baseball player from the time he was a little boy. He'd often watch the big leaguers play and he would dream of being one of them.

It's good to dream. It makes you work harder to try to make the dream come true. Hank Aaron worked very hard. He practiced every day and made his dream come true.

Hank Aaron—at bat.

Hank has been a big leaguer since 1954. He has set many baseball records. His lifetime batting average is over .300. He is one of a few players with more than 3,000 base hits. He has hit more home runs than any player in history except Babe Ruth.

Babe Ruth belted 714 homers during his long career with the New York Yankees. Hank Aaron had hit 673 before the start of the 1973 season. Most experts think that Hank will break Babe Ruth's

Babe Ruth—at bat.

home run record. If he does, it will be one of the greatest feats in sports history.

Hank Aaron was born in Mobile, Alabama, on February 5, 1934. His father and mother lived in Mobile because Mr. Aaron had a job there. He was a boilermaker's assistant. Mr. Aaron was luckier than many black men in Mobile. Jobs were hard to find. But he had seven children to support and he worked very hard.

Young Hank stayed close to home. He didn't like to play with a lot of boys. He had just one or two friends in the neighborhood, and often spent much of his time alone in his back yard.

"Henry stayed by himself for hours on end when he was about five years old," his mother said. "He'd just play in the yard, spinning his top, and watching it. I remember one day I walked out there and he was playing with the top, all right. Only he was hitting it with a baseball bat."

A few years later, Hank saw major league baseball for the first time. The big league teams practiced for the season in Florida. The weather was warm there in the spring. Then they took the train north. On the way, they stopped in many cities and played a game in each one. Mobile was a regular stop.

Hank was eight years old at the time.

He would go out to Hartwell Field and sit in the bleachers when the big league teams played. He watched Joe DiMaggio and Stan Musial. They set a lot of baseball records. Someday, Hank would break many of them.

He loved the way Joe DiMaggio played the outfield and hit the ball. He thought to himself:

"I'd like to play baseball like Joe when I grow up."

But Hank didn't even like playing ball with the other boys when he was eight. He stayed by himself. Sometimes he played catch with his older brother, and sometimes with his father and uncle. But Mr. Aaron couldn't play with his son very often. He worked hard and was away from home most days. Hank remembers well.

"My Daddy worked very hard," Hank said. "He always did. He wasn't a lazy man at all. I heard he was a good ballplayer when he was younger, and I guess that's where I get some of my ability from."

Mr. and Mrs. Aaron kept a close watch on their young son. They didn't want him to get into any trouble. Sometimes Hank skipped school to watch the major leaguers play. When his parents found out, they scolded him. They told him it was wrong to skip school, and education was very important.

One time, Mr. Aaron told his young son:

"I give you fifty cents to take to school every day for your lunch and other things," Mr. Aaron said. "But I only take twenty-five cents to work with me. That's because it's worth more to me to see you get an education than it is for me to eat."

Hank listened to his father that day. He knew his father was right. He promised to try harder and not to skip school. But he already loved baseball. It was more important to him than anything else.

From 1943 to 1945, many of the star ballplayers were in the Army and Navy, fighting in World War II. They all returned from the war in 1946 and 1947, and Hank rushed out to Hartwell Field to watch them play again. He was 13 now, and loved to see DiMaggio and the others more than ever.

There was another ballplayer that Hank wanted to watch. He was Jackie Robinson, and he played for the Brooklyn Dodgers of the National League. There was a special reason why young Hank wanted to watch Jackie Robinson play.

Jackie Robinson came to the major leagues in 1947. Before that, no black man had ever played baseball in the major leagues. It is hard to believe now, but it is true. Until 1947, black ballplayers had to play in special Negro Leagues. They didn't make much money. They had to travel in old buses and play in small, broken-down ballparks.

There were some great baseball players in the Negro Leagues. Josh Gibson and Satchel Paige were two of them. They might have been as great as Babe Ruth and Sandy Koufax if they had been allowed to play in the major leagues. Today the great Negro League players are being elected to baseball's Hall of Fame. For years, though, nobody knew them. They played the game because they loved it. But it wasn't easy for them.

It took the great courage of two men to get black ballplayers into the major leagues. One of the men was Branch Rickey, a white man in charge of the Brooklyn baseball club. The other was

Jackie Robinson, a black man, and a great athlete.

Mr. Rickey knew it was shameful that blacks couldn't play big league baseball. He decided that his team would be the first to have a black ballplayer. He picked Robinson for several reasons. First, he knew that Jackie was a great ballplayer and would do very well in the major leagues. He also knew that Jackie was a very intelligent man. He could face the many problems that would come his way.

Branch Rickey was right. Jackie Robinson played very well when he joined the Dodgers. He had to listen to many insults from fans and from other players who didn't think a black man should be allowed to play in the big leagues.

But Jackie Robinson stood up to everything and became a star. In the next few years, other black players entered the big leagues. The courage of Robinson and Rickey had paved the way. Young boys like Hank Aaron were filled with new hope.

When Jackie Robinson first played for the Dodgers, Hank was just 13. But he was already becoming a good ballplayer. He played mostly softball then, and hit the ball better than anyone else his age in Mobile.

People wondered how Hank hit so well. He didn't even hold the bat correctly. He batted cross-handed. That meant he held his left hand above his right on the bat. Right-handed batters like Hank are supposed to hold their right hand above the left. He did it backwards, yet he still hit better than anyone else. That's how good he was.

In 1949, Hank entered Central High School. He played hardball for the first time. He still hit cross-handed, but it didn't matter. He was good. He caught and played shortstop, and was the best player in the school.

Blacks still had to go to separate schools in those days. But Hank didn't mind. He was playing baseball and he was happy. For two straight years, he led his team to the Negro High School Championship of Mobile.

Central wasn't the only team he played for. About the same time he entered high school, a man named Ed Scott approached him with a question.

"How would you like to make some money, Aaron?" he asked.

Hank didn't know what to think. But when Scott said, "Playing baseball!" Hank's ears perked up.

Scott wanted Hank to play for the Mobile Black Bears. They were the best semi-pro team in town. A player on a semi-pro team gets some money for playing. But it's not much money. The team plays only once or twice a week. That's why it's called semi-pro and not a full professional team.

But the Black Bears were good. They played a lot of the teams in the area. Sometimes they played traveling teams in the Negro Leagues, such as the Indianapolis Clowns and Kansas City Monarchs. Hank had to convince his mother that it was all right for him to play. Finally she said he could.

The Bears played ball in a town called Prichard, which was near Mobile. The players made from three to five dollars a game. A player had to do real well to earn five dollars. Sometimes Hank did so well that he was paid ten dollars for the game, more than anyone else ever got.

Hank also went to his first big league tryout when he was 15. The Brooklyn Dodgers held a special camp in Mobile so they could look at the local boys. Hank didn't have enough confidence. The older boys pushed him out of the way. He never got a chance to show how well he could hit and field. He cried when he got home that night. He knew he'd have to have more confidence if he ever wanted to play in the big leagues.

CHAPTER 2

For two years, Hank was a super player for the Mobile Black Bears. Then, in the summer of 1950, the Bears scheduled a game with the Indianapolis Clowns. The Clowns were one of the most famous teams in the Negro Leagues.

Hank had a great day. He slammed two singles and a double. He also made some great plays in the field. A man named Bunny Downs, who managed the

Clowns on the road, approached the young player after the game.

"You're a good ballplayer, kid," Downs snapped. "How would you like to play baseball for the Indianapolis Clowns?"

Hank couldn't believe his ears. He tried to hide his excitement.

"I don't see why not," he answered.

"Good," Downs said. "You'll hear from me soon. I'll send you a contract when you graduate from high school."

Hank had a year of school left. His parents had taken him out of Central High and sent him to the Josephine Allen Institute for his senior year. They thought that was a better school and would help Hank get into college.

All that year, Hank wondered if he'd ever hear from Downs again. But sure enough, a few weeks after he graduated from Josephine Allen in June of 1951, he received a contract offering him $200 a month to play for the Clowns. If he signed it, he'd be a professional ballplayer at last.

There was just one problem. Hank's parents didn't understand what it really meant to be a baseball player. They didn't know anything about life in the big leagues. They wondered whether Hank could make good playing ball. They thought he should go to college.

It took a long time, but Hank finally talked his parents into letting him play for the Indianapolis Clowns. Then one day in May of 1952, Hank Aaron left home for the first time.

"I was worried about him," said his mother. "He was a quiet boy who loved to stay home. Now he was going out on his own. I knew he'd be homesick. But I also knew that he had to go."

At the railroad station, Hank and his mother hugged each other. Then Hank got on the train and started for Winston Salem, North Carolina, where the Clowns were training. All he had with him were two pairs of pants, two sandwiches, and two dollars. But his baseball career had begun.

At first, Hank was sorry that he had left home. He was the youngest player in the training camp. The older players didn't treat him well. They were afraid of losing their jobs. Very few even talked to him.

"Henry used to call us up all the time," said Mrs. Aaron. "He was homesick, just like I knew he'd be. He said the older players were riding him a lot. They were giving him a hard time. He thought maybe he should come home.

"I really didn't know what to say to him. So I put his brother on the phone. Herbert was six years older than Henry and I knew Henry would listen to him."

Mrs. Aaron was right. Herbert told Hank to stay with the team. He said that Hank had wanted to play baseball for a long time. He shouldn't give up his big chance so soon. Hank agreed. He said he'd stay with the Clowns.

When Hank first joined the team, he still hit cross-handed. The team's owner, Syd Pollock, told him he'd never make the majors hitting that way. So Hank worked hard to break his old habit. Before long he was slamming solid line drives and long home runs. He saw how much more power he had hitting the correct way. Pretty soon, he never hit cross-handed again.

His batting style has never changed since then. Hank always stays relaxed at the plate. His feet are spread slightly, the left foot a little closer to the plate. That's called a closed stance. The bat is held fairly high, just above the shoulder. The right elbow is cocked upward. Most of Hank's power comes from his very fast and very strong wrists. They give the bat its snap. Some say Hank has the quickest and strongest wrists ever.

Pretty soon, other people were noticing the young shortstop. First the New York Giants were interested. Then the Boston Braves heard about Aaron. One day the Braves sent a scout to watch Hank play. His name was Dewey Griggs.

That day, Hank got seven hits in nine tries. Two of the hits were home runs. In the field, Hank started five double plays. Griggs's eyes almost popped out of his head.

Soon, both the Braves and the Giants were offering money to young Hank Aaron. The Braves offered $350 a month. They wanted Hank to play in the Class C league. The Giants wanted to send him to a Class A team, a high league.

But they would only pay $300 a month. People advised him to go to the Braves' Class C team in Eau Claire, Wisconsin. Hank thought the Braves were being fairer than the Giants, so he signed.

People don't mention it very often, but if the Giants had made a better offer to Hank, he and Willie Mays would have been teammates down through the years. What a combination that would have been!

But Hank signed with the Braves. Though some young ballplayers were already getting "bonuses," large sums of money to sign, Hank got none. The Clowns gave him a handshake and a cardboard suitcase. But the Braves paid the Clowns $10,000 for Hank's contract.

When he went to Eau Claire to join his new team, Hank had another experience. He took his first airplane ride. He was scared stiff and admitted it. But once he got to Eau Claire, the team traveled by car. That was better than the bus rides with the Clowns.

Hank played 87 games for Eau Claire during the 1952 season. He had a very good batting average of .336. He also hit nine home runs and had 61 runs batted in. And he stole 25 bases. There was nothing he couldn't do on the ballfield. It was a great year. Hank was on the all-star team. He was voted the league's Rookie of the Year, and he finished second in the batting race.

Looking back now, Hank says 1952 was his hardest year in baseball.

"That Northern League pitching was really tough," he recalled. "It was certainly the toughest ball I'd ever played to that time. But I was getting older and I had more confidence than ever before."

Hank must have looked good. When the season ended, his manager at Eau

Claire, Billy Adair, told him he would be going to a Class A team in the South Atlantic League. The league was nicknamed the Sally League and had teams all over the deep south. Hank's team was in Jacksonville, Florida.

It was an exciting time for Hank. He found out that he would be one of the first black men ever to play in the Sally League. Hank knew there might be some trouble from people who wanted the league to keep black players out. But he wanted to play in the Sally League. It would bring him a step closer to the major leagues.

As it turned out, there were two other blacks at Jacksonville. They were Felix Mantilla, who was a Puerto Rican, and Horace Garner. Mantilla was a shortstop, expected to make the majors at that position. Hank was the second baseman.

The three blacks were not allowed to

Hank and his wife, Barbara, talking to reporters at a press conference in 1966.

live with the rest of the team. The white players all stayed at the team hotel, but Hank, Mantilla and Garner had to stay in private black homes. In a funny sort of way, it worked out well. Hank and the other blacks had home-cooked meals and comfortable beds. It was better than a hotel.

When someone once asked Hank about being one of the first blacks in the Sally League, he said:

"There's only one way to break the color line, and that is to play good. If you play really good, half the people don't remember what color you are."

Hank played good, all right. He hit better than anyone else in the league. Most people forgot about his color. But in some towns he still had trouble. There was one big southern city where he was always called "nigger." But he answered them with his home run bat.

In just 137 games, Hank hit .362, which led the league. He belted out 22 homers and drove in 125 runs. He had 208 base hits. When it all ended, he was voted Most Valuable Player in the Sally League for the 1953 season. He was on the brink of becoming a big leaguer.

There was another important event in Hank's life that year. He met a pretty girl named Barbara Lucas. She was a business student at Florida A & M University. They started dating and soon fell in love. On October 6, 1953, they were married.

Two days later, Hank and Barbara were on their way to Puerto Rico. It was a combination honeymoon and work trip. Hank's manager at Jacksonville, Ben Geraghty, told him the Braves wanted him to learn to play the outfield. If he did, he'd have a real chance to play in the major leagues the next year. So he went to Puerto Rico and learned to play the outfield.

Hank couldn't wait for spring training to begin. He was assigned to the Braves' Triple A Farm club at Toledo, but he would train with the Braves themselves at Bradenton, Florida. It was a big thrill for him, but he still didn't think he would make the Braves. After all, he was just 20 years old.

In 1954, the Braves were considered an up-and-coming team. They had moved from Boston to Milwaukee, and had some fine performers ready to charm fans in their new city.

But the team needed additional talent. Manager Charlie Grimm and General Manager John Quinn wanted a left-fielder and a second baseman. The team made two trades in the spring of 1954 to try to solve the problem.

One of the trades was with the New York Giants, and a leftfielder named Bobby Thomson came to the Braves. Thomson was the hero of the Giants' 1951 pennant win, and he was considered a good hitter. When the Braves traded for Thomson, Hank was sure he was headed back to the minors.

Early in the exhibition season, Hank didn't play much. He would pinch-hit late in the games, and do nothing else. He wasn't getting much of a chance to show how he could play the outfield. It was disappointing, but Hank expected it. Then, on March 14, something happened that changed everything.

The Braves were playing the New York Yankees. Hank had pinch-hit and had taken a shower. He was standing under the bleachers, drinking a Coke, and watching the ballgame. Bobby

Thomson was up. He hit a long drive to left. Bobby ran hard around first and went sliding into second. He didn't get up.

All the Braves gathered around their new player. Hank didn't know what was happening. He was still standing there when they carried Thomson past him on a stretcher. Hank saw Thomson's face. It was twisted with pain. Later he found out that Bobby Thomson's ankle was broken.

People tried to guess who'd take Thomson's place. There were three or four players in the running. But no one thought it would be young Hank Aaron.

When Manager Charlie Grimm approached Hank the next morning, no one knew what was going to happen. Then, suddenly, Grimm picked up Hank's glove and tossed it to him.

"Here, kid. You're my new leftfielder. The job's yours until someone takes it away from you."

Hank just stood there with his mouth open. It was the last thing he had expected. Even though Thomson was out of the lineup, Hank thought veteran Jim Pendleton would get the call. He still thought he'd be sent to the minors.

Though Hank was just 20 years old, he was a full-grown man. Hank stands six feet tall and weighs 180 pounds. He's always played at that weight and has never been fat or out of shape. It's one of the reasons he's played so well down through the years.

Right before the start of the season, General Manager John Quinn made it official. He told Hank that the Braves had purchased his contract from Toledo. Hank looked at the paper in front of him, took a pen, and signed. When he thinks back on that scene today, he laughs out loud.

"I was so happy to be in the big leagues that I just signed the contract," he says. "I didn't know what the salary was. I trusted John Quinn and didn't even care about the rest."

CHAPTER 3

The day after Hank signed his contract, he trotted out to left field. The Braves were playing the Cincinnati Reds. Hank wasn't nervous, but he was excited. The dream he had as a young boy in Mobile was coming true. He had always told his parents and friends that he would play in the big leagues. And here he was, standing out in left field for the Milwaukee Braves.

Hank didn't get any hits that day. He says he was trying too hard. But he didn't have to worry. Manager Grimm was going to give him a full chance to win the job. In fact, Grimm thought so much of the young outfielder that he told the press:

"Hank's not the spectacular type. He makes everything look easy out there. So we're not going to try to make another Willie Mays out of him. But mark my words, he'll be around a long time after Willie's gone."

It wasn't long before Hank started hitting the ball. On April 23, he got his first major league home run off Vic Raschi of the Cardinals. Two days later he belted another, this time off Stu Miller. Young Hank had hit two home runs off smart, veteran pitchers. He felt proud. He knew he could hit major league pitching, and he knew he had the power to hit home runs.

Hank played in almost every game for most of the season. He was doing well for a rookie, and the team was still in the pennant race. On September 5, the Braves were just five games out of first place behind the Brooklyn Dodgers.

The Braves were playing a doubleheader at Cincinnati. Hank didn't play in the first game. Bobby Thomson, the man who had broken his ankle in spring training, started in left field. Hank went in as a pinch runner in the seventh inning, and later slammed a double. The Braves won. In the second game, Hank got four more hits and really felt great.

But his last hit was one he'll never forget. It was a long triple to deep centerfield, and Hank ran hard around the bases. Coming into third, he saw the coach signal for a slide and he hit the dirt. His left leg got caught in the ground

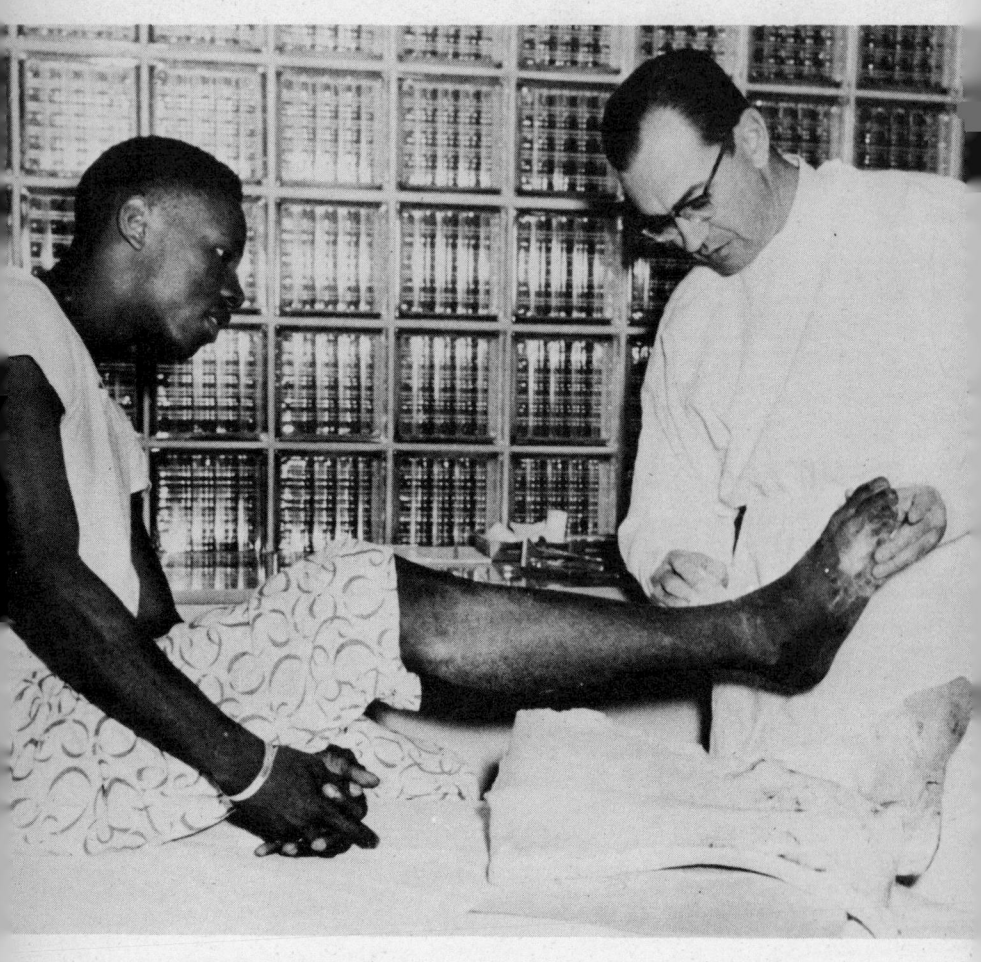

Here's the ankle that put Hank out of action. The doctor has just removed the cast.

and he fell heavily on his right leg. He felt pain and couldn't stand up.

It was hard to believe. One broken ankle (Bobby Thomson's) put Hank in the lineup. And now another broken ankle (his own) would take him out. The doctors had to operate and put a pin in the ankle to help it heal. Hank was in the hospital for three weeks. He wouldn't play ball again the rest of the season.

Hank had a good rookie season. He played in 122 games, collected 131 hits, belted 13 homers, and knocked in 69 runs. His batting average was a solid .280. But he wasn't satisfied.

"I'm very happy that I got the chance to play in the big leagues," Hank told a reporter. "But I feel I should have done better on the field."

Then the reporter told Hank he had done better than many baseball greats the first year. Players like Ty Cobb, Rogers Hornsby, and Willie Mays hadn't hit as well as Hank when they were rookies.

"Yeah, maybe," Hank replied. "But I've been hitting .340 all my life. I was hitting over .400 with the Indianapolis Clowns. So hitting .280, even with the Braves, doesn't make me feel that good. I'll do better next year."

When he reported to the Braves' training camp in 1955, something new was awaiting him. It was uniform number 44. During his rookie year, Hank told club officials that he didn't like the number "5" that was assigned to him. For some reason, he liked double numbers like "22," "33," or "44." So the team decided to make the young slugger happy. Now he was number "44." He'd wear that uniform for a long time.

In 1955, Hank made good on his promise to do better. Playing in all but one game, he socked out 189 hits, slammed 27 homers, and drove in 106 runs. In addition, he led the league in doubles with 37, and batted .314. He had hit better than .300 for the first time. He also made the all-star team for the first time.

But the Braves were second best again. When 1956 rolled around, Hank and his teammates were determined to go after the pennant.

All year the Braves and the Brooklyn Dodgers battled for first place. The Braves were in front for 126 days, while the Dodgers were first for just 17 days. But on the last day of the year the Dodgers clinched the pennant and the Braves were second once more. The Milwaukee owners were getting fed up. During the season they fired Manager Charlie Grimm and replaced him with tough Fred Haney. When they lost it on the last day, the players said next year would be the one.

As for Hank, he was becoming one of the stars of the National League. He proved himself again as a hitter by leading the league with a .328 average. It was his best yet. He also led the league in hits with 200, in doubles with 34, and in total bases with 340. His 26 homers and 92 RBI's were also good marks.

He was playing right field now, and playing it well. In the lineup every day, he was a smooth player. He made difficult plays look easy. But he played the outfield as well as anyone and was a great hitter. In his quiet way he was playing the game as it was supposed to be played.

More than two million fans had come to Milwaukee County Stadium to see the

Braves that year. They saw two 20-game winners in Warren Spahn and Lew Burdette. Hank, Ed Mathews, and Joe Adcock were all top sluggers. But there was no pennant. Hank said it was the first time he really felt how much it hurt to lose.

The Braves started working hard in spring training the next year. They were determined to win. The work paid off. The team won nine of its first 10 games and were off and running. But soon after came another slump. By June, it was obvious that some changes had to be made. The result was a trade that brought veteran second baseman Red Schoendienst to the Braves from the Giants.

Schoendienst pulled the team together. The switch-hitting redhead was a smooth fielder and tough hitter. When he came to the Braves, Manager Haney put him in the second spot in the lineup. The

Ed Mathews, Warren Spahn and Hank Aaron—three great Braves.

second hitter was moved into the fourth spot. His name: Hank Aaron.

Now Hank was batting "clean-up," the nickname given to the fourth hitter. He would have a chance to drive in more runs since the clean-up hitter often comes to bat with men on base. It showed again that Hank was becoming the biggest man in the Braves' attack.

Hank was playing like a real superstar. Later that year centerfielder Bill Bruton got hurt. Hank again showed he was a good all-around player. He volunteered to move from right field to center field. It wasn't easy. He had more responsibility in the field, since the centerfielder has more territory to cover. Also, the Braves' two other outfielders were slow. The change made it harder for him to concentrate at the plate.

The Braves stayed in first place.

Schoendienst plugged up the infield, and Aaron did the same for the outfield after Bruton was hurt. They were closer to the pennant than ever before. On the night of September 23, 1957, the Braves were playing the Cardinals with a chance to win it.

The game went into the 11th inning with the score tied. Hank came up against a pitcher named Billy Muffett. There was one man on base.

Hank waited for a pitch he liked. When he got it, he snapped his powerful wrists and the ball rocketed out toward center field. It cleared the fence and the Braves had won the National League pennant. The city of Milwaukee went wild. All his teammates mobbed Hank. They carried him off the field. He was a hero. He said it was the happiest moment of his life.

What a season it had been! Hank led

the league in homers with 44, and in runs batted in with 132. His .322 batting average was near the top of the league. After the season he was named the National League's Most Valuable Player. Hank Aaron was now a real superstar.

CHAPTER 4

The World Series of 1957 was the thrill of a lifetime for Hank. It's the goal of every big league ballplayer. The Braves were facing the powerful New York Yankees. Most people thought the Yanks would win. They usually did.

The New Yorkers had many star players. Men like Mickey Mantle, Yogi Berra, Hank Bauer, and Whitey Ford were all very good.

Ford was pitching against Warren Spahn in the first game. It took place at Yankee Stadium on October 2, 1957. Hank was nervous as he looked up at the large crowd of 70,000 fans. But he knew that once the game started, he'd feel better.

Neither team scored in the first four innings. A double by Hank Bauer brought home the first Yankee run in the fifth. The Yanks got two more runs in the sixth and led, 3–0. The Braves put two men on with none out in the sixth. Now Hank was up. Most people thought Manager Haney would tell Hank to bunt. But he didn't.

Hank waited for a good pitch. But the cagey Ford threw a sharp curve that broke over the plate. Hank was called out on strikes, and the Yanks went on to win the first game.

Later, Manager Haney was asked why he didn't have Hank bunt.

"Listen," he growled. "I don't bunt, especially away from home and with my best hitter up."

That showed how much faith the manager had in Hank. And although Hank did get a hit later, he was sorry that he struck out in the sixth. He was determined to do better in the upcoming games.

In the second inning of the second game, Hank swung at a fastball thrown by the Yankees' Bobby Shantz. He felt the ball jump off his bat and started running. The ball carried over Mantle's head in deep center. Hank ran hard. He slid into third base with a triple. The long hit felt good to him.

When Joe Adcock singled, Hank crossed the plate to give the Braves a 1–0 lead. The Yanks tied the score in the second, but the Braves went on to win the game, 4–2. Righthander Lew Burdette pitched a great game. Now the series was tied at one game each. Hank didn't get any other hits. But he knew he could hit the Yankee pitching. He was looking forward to game three at Milwaukee.

The third game was a disaster for the Braves. The Milwaukee pitchers were wild. They walked 11 Yankees. The New Yorkers scored three runs in the first inning, two in the third, and two more in the fourth. It was a 7–1 game when Hank came up with one man on base in the fifth.

He was facing big righthander Don Larsen. He waited patiently. Larsen threw a fastball and Hank snapped his strong wrists. The ball flew off his bat. It was high and deep to left. Hank watched it drop into the stands for his first World Series home run. He had mixed feelings as he trotted around the bases. He was happy he hit a homer, but his team was still behind, 7–3.

Then the Yanks exploded for five more runs in the seventh. They had a huge 12–3 lead. Hank's homer was wasted. New York won the game and had a 2–1 lead. Everyone said the Braves were finished.

Hank had made two hits, including the homer. He also made a sensational, sliding catch of a line drive. Though the Braves lost, many people thought Hank was the best player on the field.

The Braves had to win the fourth game. When the Yanks took a 1–0 lead in the first, it looked bleak. But in the fourth, the Braves came back. Shortstop Johnny Logan walked, and Mathews doubled to right. Now Hank was up

Hank's sensational catch in the third game. The umpires decided he caught it.

again. He was facing Yankee righthander Tom Sturdivant. Sturdivant threw a knuckleball, a strange pitch that is very difficult to hit.

But Hank was ready. He stepped into the pitch and hit a long drive to left field. The ball cleared the barrier for another home run. This time Hank's hit put the Braves in front, 3–1. His teammates congratulated him in the dugout. He was having a great world series.

But the Yanks weren't through. They tied the game in the ninth on a homer by Elston Howard. Then they took a 5–4 lead in the tenth. But the Braves rallied in the last of the tenth. Eddie Mathews hit a homer and Milwaukee won, 7–5. The series was tied again.

In the fifth game, Burdette was pitching against Ford. Both hurlers were great. Neither team could score a run. Then in the sixth inning, Mathews got an infield hit. Now Hank was up. He knew he had to keep the rally going. He swung easily at an outside curve, and blooped a single to right field. Then Joe Adcock hit a single and the Braves had a run. Burdette pitched a shutout. Milwaukee won, 1–0, and took a 3–2 lead in the series.

Hank was really excited now. He had always wanted to play on a championship team. Now he had his chance. In the sixth game, Hank came up in the seventh inning with the Yanks ahead, 2–1. Facing Bob Turley, Hank swung at a fastball and hit a tremendous drive to left. It was his third home run and it tied the ballgame.

"Now we can win it," he thought as he rounded the bases.

But the Yanks didn't like to lose, either. Hank Bauer hit a home run in the same inning, and the New Yorkers had tied the series with a 3–2 win. The team that won the next game would win the series.

There was a great deal of tension before the game. Another big crowd was at Yankee Stadium to root for the Yanks. But Hank wasn't nervous anymore. He was used to the pressure now. He was confident the Braves would win. Burdette would pitch for the Braves against Don Larsen of the Yankees.

In the third inning, the Braves got two runs on a double by Mathews. The Yankees brought in a new pitcher, Bobby Shantz. Hank was up. He wasted no time, slamming a base hit to center. Mathews scored the third Milwaukee run of the game. Another single and an infield out brought Hank home with the fourth Milwaukee run.

Hank jumped on home plate with both feet. It was as if he knew the Yanks wouldn't catch the Braves now. He was right. Catcher Del Crandall belted a homer in the eighth. Burdette pitched his second shutout, and the Braves won the game, 5–0. They were champions of the baseball world.

Lew Burdette was the Braves' pitching star. And the best hitter in the series was Hank Aaron. He had shown the baseball world that he was a real star. With the pressure on, Hank had 11 hits in seven games. That was just one short of the record. He batted .393, and led both teams with three homers and seven runs batted in. It was the happiest moment of his career.

But soon it was spring again and a new season. Hank batted .326 in 1958, as the Braves won another pennant with relative ease. It was hard to believe that once again Milwaukee would face New York for the championship.

This time it started as if the Braves would win easily. They won the first game, 4–3, in ten innings. Hank's double in the eighth brought home the tying run. Then in the second game, Milwaukee exploded for 13 runs, with Hank getting two more hits.

But it was the Yanks' turn to come back. They won the third game, 4–0, behind Don Larsen. Then Warren Spahn went out and blanked the Yanks, 3–0. Hank had two more hits in that one, and the Braves led, three games to one. It looked as though the Yanks were finished.

Only the Braves couldn't win another game. Bob Turley pitched a shutout in game five. Then the Yanks won the sixth game. Once again, the series would be decided in the final game. And once again Lew Burdette took to the mound against Don Larsen.

The big righthander didn't pitch very well. It was a 2–2 game going into the eighth, but the Yanks got four big runs and went on to win the game, 6–2, and the series.

It was a disappointing series for Hank. He was the Braves' leader again with nine hits in 27 trips for a .333 average. But he failed to hit a home run. And he only drove in two runs. He knew that he didn't get the big hits as he had the year before. He told reporters that he'd make up for it the next year.

He sure did. Hank had one of his greatest seasons in 1959. He won his second batting title with a .355 average. He also led the league in hits with 223 and in total bases with 400. In addition, he had 39 homers and 123 RBI's. But it wasn't good enough.

The Braves tied the Dodgers for the pennant. There was a special playoff, and the Dodgers won two straight games to take the pennant. Hank had a great year, but he was sad that his team had not won.

"We lost on the last day of the season in 1956," he said, "and in a playoff in 1959. With a little more luck, we could have won four straight pennants."

During the next four seasons, Hank continued to batter National League pitching. He hit 40, 34, 45, and 44 homers. He also drove in 126, 120, 128, and 130 runs in those years (1960–63). What's more, he hit over .300 in three of those seasons.

The Braves had a new manager, a man named Bobby Bragan. Bragan was a fiery leader who liked to get the most out of his players. He approached Hank.

"You're a complete ballplayer," he told the superstar. "But you're not using all your talents. I think you should run the bases more."

Hank said he'd give it a try. He had never stolen many bases before, but when he started running, he was tough to stop. The Braves had a slugging team, so Hank didn't run all that much. But when he did, he was as good as they come.

In 1963, Hank was the National League's Player of the Year. He also became just the fifth man in baseball history to hit more than 30 homers (he had 44) and steal more than 30 bases (he stole 31) in the same season. Base stealers are not usually home-run hitters. But Hank was. He led the league in homers that year. He was also tops in runs batted in with 130, in hits with 201, and in total bases. It was his tenth year in the major leagues.

Hank's reputation continued to grow.

Throughout the year, other players always got more publicity than Hank. Now, baseball people were saying that Hank was as good as anyone else in the game.

CHAPTER 5

The 1964 and 1965 seasons were not great by Hank's usual standards. He hit over .300 both years (.328 and .318), but he didn't hit as many homers. He didn't realize it, but the other Braves were slipping badly.

Most of the Milwaukee stars during the pennant years were older than Hank. And now when Hank was in his prime, players like Spahn, Burdette, Mathews,

Waiting for a big one.

Logan, Adcock, and Crandall couldn't play as well as they once did. Some of them had been traded away. New players were coming and going. The team had several new managers. Each one had his own system, and changed the players some more. Even the fans booed the team. Only Hank remained a favorite and a star.

Finally, the team owners decided to do something about it. They decided to move the team out of Milwaukee. Its new home was in Atlanta, Georgia. So when the 1966 season opened, Hank Aaron pulled on his number "44" jersey for the Atlanta Braves. It was the team's third city.

It didn't make any difference to Hank. He was swinging for the fences to please his new fans. When the season ended, Hank had 44 home runs and 127 runs batted in. But his batting average slipped

A new home plate doesn't stop the home runs.

to .279, the poorest of his career. He didn't like that.

"I don't know what happened," he says. "I think I was just trying to hit too many home runs for the new fans. I know I'm not a .279 hitter."

The Braves knew how good Hank was. Before the 1967 season started, they rewarded him with a two-year contract, giving him $100,000 each year. It was about time. Other superstars were making that much, and Hank was certainly as good as any of them. He was very happy.

Up to now, Hank really hadn't been thought of as a great home run hitter. He never had a "big" homer year, that is, 50 or 55 homers. But he was always around the 40 mark, and the numbers were adding up.

On April 20, 1966, he hit his 400th homer off Bo Belinsky of Philadelphia.

And later in the year, he and teammate Eddie Mathews set a record for the most home runs by two players on the same team. The record was held by Babe Ruth and Lou Gehrig.

The next year Hank hit 39 (and got his average over .300 again). Then in 1968, he belted number 500 off Mike McCormick of the Giants. Hank was now 34 years old and entering a select group of great home run hitters. He had always trailed hitters like Mickey Mantle and Willie Mays. But now he was gaining on them. He loved the park in Atlanta and he loved his new fans.

"I've never had an ovation like the one when I hit my 500th homer," he said. "It was really great."

And other players were saying things about Hank Aaron that indicated he was an all-time great. Sandy Koufax, the great Dodger lefthander, said:

Hank scores.

Hank leaps high and crashes into the right field wall in the eighth inning to steal a three run homer from Dick Dietz of the San Francisco Giants, July 1968. The Braves won, 5–1.

"Hank is the toughest in the league. There's no way you can pitch him when he's hot."

The Giants' star hurler Juan Marichal said it another way. Hank had just gotten four hits off him and stolen two bases.

"That man," said Juan, "if he doesn't beat you one way, he beats you another."

And a veteran second-string catcher, Charlie Lau, who had had plenty of time to watch the stars in both leagues, said:

"I've seen every superstar of recent years. Mantle, Mays, Kaline, Mathews, Clemente—all of them—and Aaron's the best. He beats you hitting, running, fielding, and stealing. There's nothing he can't do."

It is true. But when people would talk to Hank about his records, he'd just laugh.

"Setting records means you're getting old," he would say.

Hank was getting on. He began resting more. He didn't play both games of doubleheaders, and he sat out some day games that followed night games. But he kept hitting.

The Braves had a good year in '69, winning the Western Division pennant in the National League. But under the new set-up, they had to play the Eastern Division winner, the New York Mets, to get into the World Series. The Mets won, but Hank had three homers in three games. He did his best to keep his team from losing.

Hank Aaron has always taken good care of himself. He's never been hurt badly since the broken ankle his first year. He still plays at 180 pounds and stays in good condition throughout the season.

He continues to live a quiet life in Atlanta. He spends a lot of time with his

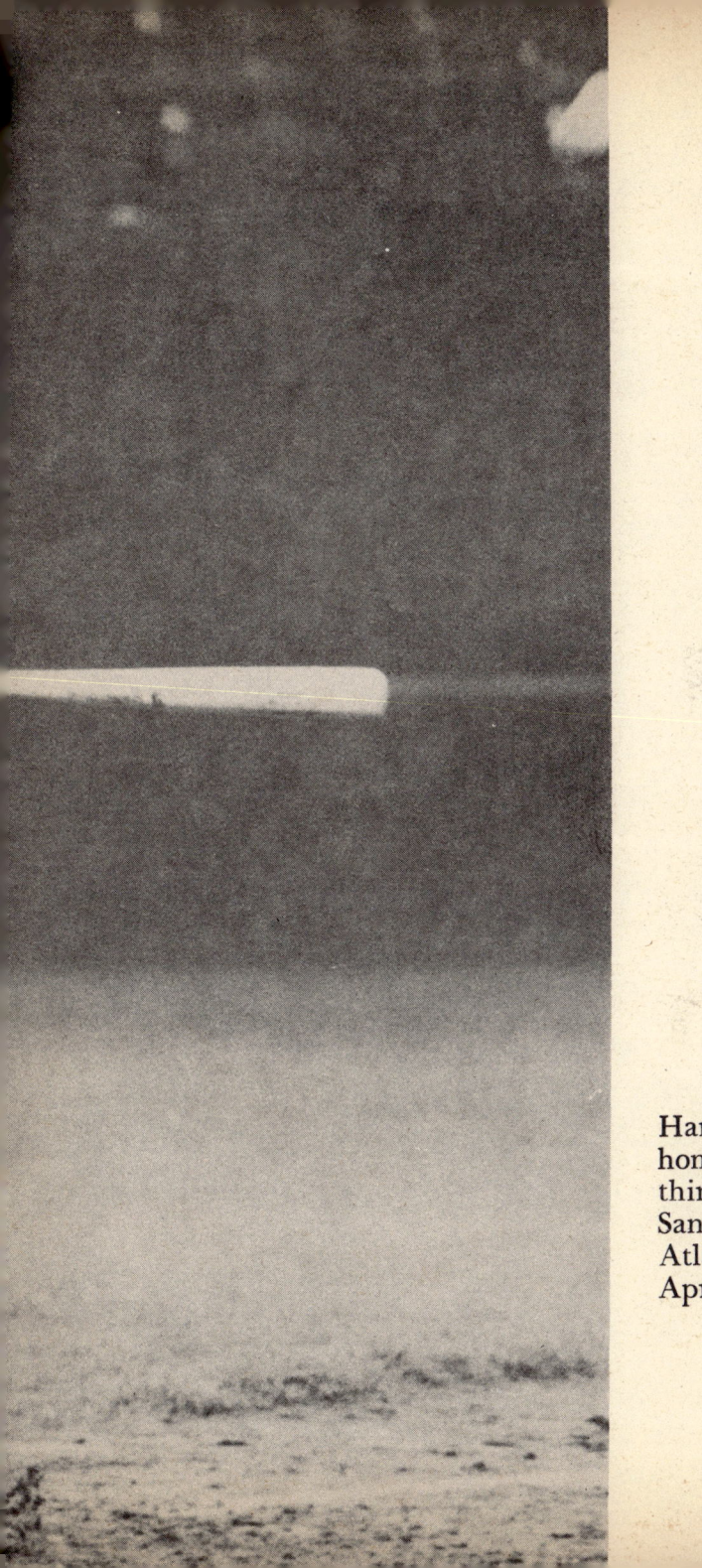

Hank's 600th homer. It was the third inning of a San Francisco–Atlanta game, April, 1971.

four children—Gail, Henry, Jr., Larry, and Dorinda. Hank loves watching the children grow up.

When Hank signed a contract before the 1972 season, he became the highest paid player in baseball history. Hank was now earning $200,000 per year.

"He deserves every penny of it," said Braves' President Bill Bartholomay.

And the experts were right about his homers. Early in the 1972 season, Hank passed the fading Mays as he cracked the 649th home run of his career. It happened on the night of June 10, at Philadelphia.

The Braves were beating the Phils handily when Hank stepped up with the bases loaded in the sixth inning. Philly hurler Wayne Twitchell was determined to get the veteran slugger out. He tried to throw a fastball past Hank. But Hank snapped his quick wrists and hit a long,

Hank signs his 1970 contract with the Atlanta Braves. The Braves' president, William C. Bartholomay, watches. This contract paid Hank $125,000 a year.

Hank heads for home with his 648th home run, the one that tied him with Willie Mays. Hank's teammate Rico Carty is waiting to shake Hank's hand. May, 1972.

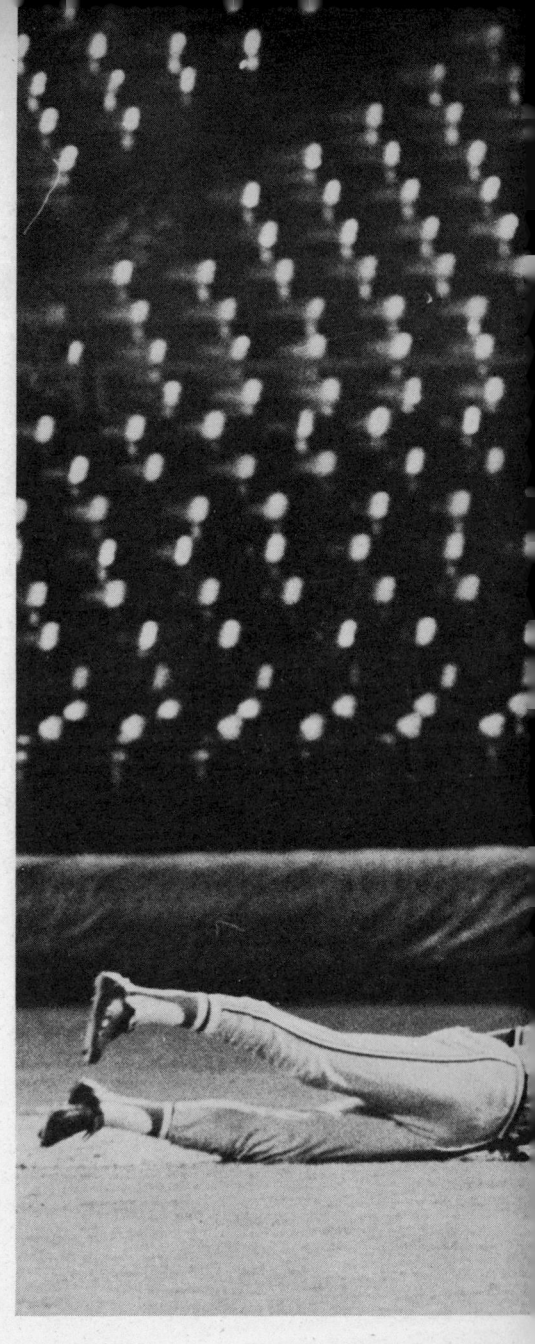

Hank plays first base.

deep drive to left field. The ball passed high over the wall for a grand slam home run.

Hank circled the bases. The other three Braves runners scored ahead of him and waited at the plate to shake his hand. It was his 10th homer of the season, and it moved him to second place on the all-time list. It was also the 14th grand slammer of his career. And that tied him for the National League record with the late Gil Hodges.

He could still hammer the ball, all right. And when Hank finished the 1972 season with 673 home runs, he was well within striking distance of the Babe.

Many people thought Hank would have a hard time in 1973 because he was 39 years old. That is very old for a baseball player. They thought he could only hit about 25 home runs.

But he fooled them. He had his home run swing right from the beginning of the year. He reached the 700 mark soon after the All-Star Game, and it looked as if he might break Babe Ruth's record of 714 before the year was over.

Hank hit better than anyone in the league during the second half of the season. With just six games left he belted his 712th homer off Dave Roberts of Houston. Then he hit number 713 off Jerry Reuss of Houston with two games to go.

There was a lot of pressure on Hank in those final games, but it didn't bother him. He was very calm, and even though he didn't hit a homer, he got six other hits to bring his final batting average to .301.

He ended the season one homer short of Ruth's record. But he had a great year, hitting 40 home runs and driving in 96 runs. He set many more records and will play again in 1974. There won't be as much pressure because he will only have to hit two home runs to break the record.

Hank plays first base a lot now. It's easier on his legs, and lets him save himself for his batting. And as a hitter, there are many records he can break.

He is near the top of the all-time list in homers, runs batted in, games played, at-bats, runs scored, hits, total bases, extra base hits, and doubles. He'll finish his career at or near the top in most of these departments. And he'll rate as one of the all-time greats of baseball.

Some things have changed for Hank over the years. He says he's a different kind of hitter than he was as a youngster.

"I'm not as strong a hitter as I was once," he admits. "When I won the home

Hank, all but hidden behind a cloud of dust as he slides for first base.

run title with 44 in 1957, a lot of my shots were to right field. Now I pull everything to left. I guess I was a better hitter then."

The way Hank still swings the bat, many people will find that hard to believe.

In 1952, Hank Aaron was just a scared kid leaving Mobile to play ball. All he had was two pairs of pants, two dollars, and two sandwiches. He's gone on to become one of the greatest players in baseball history. And he's done it in a quiet, calm way. He just plays the game.

Someone once asked Hank how he'd like to remembered. Without hesitating, he replied:

"I don't want to be anything special or anyone special. I just want to be remembered as plain Hank Aaron."

For once, Hank Aaron was wrong. He is somebody very special.

HANK AARON

Batting

Year	Club	League	G	AB
1952	Eau Claire	Northern	87	345
1953	Jacksonville	So. Atlantic	137	574
1954	Milwaukee	National	122	468
1955	Milwaukee	National	153	602
1956	Milwaukee	National	153	609
1957	Milwaukee	National	151	615
1958	Milwaukee	National	153	601
1959	Milwaukee	National	154	629
1960	Milwaukee	National	153	590
1961	Milwaukee	National	155	603
1962	Milwaukee	National	156	592
1963	Milwaukee	National	161	631
1964	Milwaukee	National	145	570
1965	Milwaukee	National	150	570
1966	Atlanta	National	158	603
1967	Atlanta	National	155	600
1968	Atlanta	National	160	606
1969	Atlanta	National	147	547
1970	Atlanta	National	150	516
1971	Atlanta	National	139	495
1972	Atlanta	National	129	449
1973	Atlanta	National	120	392
Major League totals		20 years	2964	11288

World Series

		G	AB
1957	Milwaukee vs New York	7	28
1958	Milwaukee vs New York	7	27
World Series Totals		14	55

Championship

		G	AB
1969	Atlanta vs New York	3	14

STATISTICS

Record

R	H	HR	RBI	SB	Pct.
79	116	9	61	25	.336
115	208	22	125	13	.362
58	131	13	69	2	.280
105	189	27	106	3	.314
106	200	26	92	2	.328
118	198	44	132	1	.322
109	196	30	95	4	.326
116	223	39	123	8	.355
102	172	40	126	16	.292
115	197	34	120	21	.327
127	191	45	128	15	.323
121	201	44	130	31	.319
103	187	24	95	22	.328
109	181	32	89	24	.318
117	168	44	127	21	.279
113	184	39	109	17	.307
84	174	29	86	28	.287
100	164	44	97	9	.300
103	154	38	118	9	.298
95	162	47	118	1	.327
75	119	34	77	3	.265
84	118	40	96	1	.301
2060	3509	713	2133	238	.311

Record

5	11	3	7	0	.393
3	9	0	2	0	.333
8	20	3	9	0	.364

Series Record

3	5	3	7	0	.357